Hidden in Paris

THE COOKBOOK

EASY FRENCH COMFORT FOOD

BY THE AUTHOR OF HIDDEN IN PARIS

Recipes and images by

CORINE GANTZ

To the readers of Hidden in Paris

Table of content

Meatless

Beef, Chicken, Lamb, Pork

Fish and seafood

Desserts

Introduction

Why the Hidden in Paris cookbook?

My novel Hidden in Paris came out in March 2011. A year later I'm thrilled to be able to offer a cookbook to my readers featuring most of the recipes described in the novel.

I put this cookbook together by popular demand. Readers have e-mailed me personally, commented on my blog, and even mentioned in reviews on Amazon and elsewhere that they would love to know how to make those dishes. I take this a sign that the book made them hungry, which for a writer is a terrific compliment. It means that somehow I was able to place them in France, in that Parisian kitchen, with this neurotic woman named Annie and the people to whom she opens up her house, her kitchen, and eventually her heart.

I wrote this cookbook as a way of saying thank you to those who took a chance with an unknown writer, bought and enjoyed Hidden in Paris, spread the word, and made it a success. The validation and joy that readers have brought me have made all these years of scribbling, wringing my hands, and doubting myself worth it.

This is not going to be one of those fancy-shmancy French cookbooks, is it?

Although the idea of preparing French food at home might seem intimidating, the recipes you will find in this book are for the most part quite simple to execute. This is the kind of food you will find in people's homes, prepared for a family dinner on any given evening, not the kind you will eat in restaurants.

Since, like yourself, I have things to do, places to go, children to raise, and I'm not in the business of cooking, I favor one pot dishes; recipes prepared in fifteen minutes that I can walk away from and come back to find ready to serve an hour later. I want comfort and nutrition for the least amount of time and an even smaller amount of dirty dishes.

An entire book could be devoted to the French approach to food. For the French, eating is a sensual, mostly guilt-free experience; a necessary pleasure. French people are taught to develop their palates beginning in childhood. French eating should also be put in a social context. Shopping for ingredients, preparation, and sharing a meal are some of the most basic activities around which relationships evolve.

My approach to cooking is very much like Annie's. My food is primarily basic French comfort food. Like most French women I eat all kinds of rich foods. I eat in moderation. Except of course when I'm not in the mood for moderation. I balance any excess with a lean meal the following day: a salad, soup, and no bread. Being French, I'm truly terrible at self-deprivation, and even worse at being told what I cannot eat.

Local, fresh and unprocessed... except for the love of bouillon cubes

You will see that aside for my somewhat deplorable affection for bouillon cubes and the occasional can of crushed tomatoes when sun-filled ripe tomatoes are hard to find, all the ingredients in the following recipes are fresh, unprocessed, and purchased two days in advance at the most.

A brief history of how I came to cooking. Hint: I wasn't born with a wooden spatula in my hand.

When I moved from France to the United States at the age of 23 to follow my brand new husband, I arrived having never cooked un oeuf. Cooking was low on the list of priorities since I faced more crippling obstacles. Hardly speaking English, for example. Or being newly married to an American boy who spoke little French.

My mother is a terrific cook, yet it had never occurred to me to learn from her, or occurred to her to teach me. What would have been the point when all I needed to do was knock at *Maman*'s door when I was hungry? When I was not eating in restaurants and cafés in my neighborhood the only meal I remember preparing inside my tiny *chambre de bonne* in the sixteenth arrondissement was good rabbit pâté spread on a popular packaged toasted bread called *biscottes*.

Most French people do not venture far from the nest. They usually grow up, go to the university, and live the rest of their lives in the very region, the very town where they were born. I had no plans to live somewhere other than Paris or, for that matter, anywhere that was not a stones throw from my mother's kitchen. That is until *l'amour* threw a wrench into my plans: I fell in love with an American man.

From home sickness to home cooked meals

We met and married within a year and moved to a barely furnished house in Mill Valley, a beautiful spot in Northern California. But despite the beauty of the place, I had trouble enjoying my new life and felt homesick. Then, rapidly and painfully, very, very homesick. In Northern California nothing looked, felt or smelled even remotely like Paris. I could not work, I could not communicate. I had no friends. I felt lost in every way. To tell you the truth, I was falling hard into depression and had no words for what was happening to me. I was desperately in need of something familiar and reassuring. What I desired most, what I felt I could not live without, was the taste of home. What I was after was not just food, or even French food, but specifically my mother's cooking.

I asked my mother for her recipes but she had none, she cooked instinctively, a concept that was absolutely foreign to me. Instead she sent me a copy of the only cookbook she owned, *Les Recettes Faciles de Françoise Bernard,* which might very well be the French equivalent of Joy of Cooking.

From there, I painstakingly attempted to recreate the recipes of my childhood, a calculator and dictionary in hand, translating (as does Annie in Hidden in Paris) kilos to pounds, and liters to gallons.

Preparing food became a lifeline for me, a project, a function that gave me both purpose and satisfaction, a way to stay connected, a way to express my love. Had I gotten pregnant right away I would not have had the time to indulge in two years of culinary exploration.

Cooking while under the influence

Twenty plus years later, cooking has become a very relaxed affair for me. Chopping away while sipping red wine (strictly for health reasons) and keeping an eye on homework are what my evenings are made of. You'll find in this book that I'm silly at times in my descriptions of recipes and in my notes, because cooking should be fun. Fun to shop for, fun to prepare, and fun to eat. You can substitute all you want. Cooking is not baking. This is not a precise science. For example switch chicken with beef in the *coq au vin* recipe and ta-dah! you now have *boeuf bourguignon*. Replace the cheese and salt with chocolate and sugar in the soufflé recipe, and you now have a dessert soufflé. Replace salt and pepper with coffee extract and sugar and a béchamel sauce becomes a perfect filling for coffee éclairs.

Who took the pictures in this book? Quick what's the name of this fabulous photographer?

Cooking and writing down the recipes in this book was the easy part. The hard part was to make them look photogenic. Stews, vegetables that have cooked for hours, and brown sauces can taste amazing but look just plain awful in pictures, especially when that picture is taken with a cell phone. It was quite the learning curve to teach myself the rudiments of food photography for this book, and to learn to operate a bona fide camera and tripod. There was frustration, there were thoughts of giving up, there was that awful moment when I accidentally spilled the entire contents of a glass of red wine on a pristinely styled table where a piping hot croque monsieur awaited its moment in the spotlight. Yet I came out from the experience of putting this collection of recipes together feeling more knowledgeable about photography, more inspired about cooking and, well, fatter. French women do get fat it turns out! But mostly I became motivated to continue sharing my excitement about food through writing and photography. So, although the idea was to give something to my readers, it turns out that I am the one who is benefiting the most from the experience.

Why so vague about salt?

I apologize for being all vague and furtive about salt. There is no right and wrong way to salt a dish. I discovered this after I reduced my salt consumption to control my blood pressure. I decided to leave it mostly up to you and your diet and taste preferences by suggesting you to 'salt to taste'. Salt can always be added to people's individual plates.

There is always room for improvement

I hope you enjoyed these recipes. Please let me know your thoughts and if you have tips. E-books are easy to correct and improve. I also welcome all e-mails from all of you clever typos detectives.

Bon appétit à tous!

Corine Gantz

February 10th, 2012

Coq au vin

(Chicken in Red Wine)

...Lucas peeked over Annie's shoulder and looking into the pot. "You left the rooster's bones in?" he pointed out.

"It's chicken, " Annie said, chopping parsley at high speed.

"Coq au vin sans coq?" Rooster cooked in wine without a rooster. Lucas seemed to put a great deal of thought into his reasoning. "But then," he said, "don't you have to work around the bones as you eat? Wouldn't it be better to use a boneless rooster?

"The bones give the dish its flavor. God forbid you'd have to put in the effort and work around the bones!" Annie turned to the dark-haired woman. "Lucas was born with a silver spoon filled with boneless rooster in his mouth."

Saint Germain des Prés

Coq au Vin -- Chicken in Red Wine

Note: Perfect for beginners, because the flavor is in inverse proportion to the recipe's complexity.

The recipe calls for ½ to 1 bottle of cheap red wine. You can also use very expensive one for this recipe but few will be able to tell the difference. I personally can't, so I keep my good stuff for drinking.

Coq au Vin -- Chicken in Red Wine

Ingredients for four to six servings

8 chicken legs (drumstick and thighs)

1 tbsp table oil

½ to 1 bottle red wine (such as Pinot noir)

1 cup of pancetta cut into cube-size chunks. If not using pancetta, substitute with ¼ cup good cooking oil (safflower for example. Avoid that nasty corn oil.)

4 small peeled carrots, sliced

1 large peeled onion, thinly chopped

2 cloves of garlic (peeled and crushed)

2 shallots (peeled and thinly chopped)

1- 8 oz can crushed tomatoes or 2 fresh ripe tomatoes

¼ to 1/3 cup all-purpose flour (to thicken the sauce)

1 basket mushrooms (sliced)

½ lb baby potatoes

½ cup chopped fresh parsley

1 tsp dried or fresh thyme

1 small bay leaf

Salt and pepper to taste

Directions

1- On the stove, heat the tablespoon oil in a large pan, add the pancetta and let it melt as you stir (or go to the next step for a pork-free version). Add chopped onion, stir until the onion and shallot becomes translucent. Remove the onion from the pot and reserve.

2- In the oil or pancetta residues that remain in the pot, sauté the chicken until the skin is golden. If your pan is small you might need to do this in two batches.

3- Sprinkle flour on the browned chicken and sauté for another minute.

4- Add carrots, garlic, tomatoes, herbs (except the parsley), onion, shallot, pancetta, salt and pepper. Then, in one abandoned, reckless motion of the arm, pour in all the Pinot. If needed, add water until all the chicken is covered in liquid. Bring to a boil, then reduce to a simmer and cook gently, uncovered for 1 to 1½ hours. The liquid will evaporate and the sauce will thicken. Only cover if you feel the liquid is evaporating too quickly. The smell in the kitchen should be just about to die for by now.

5- 20 minutes before serving add the potatoes. Cover so that they cook evenly.

6- 10 minutes before serving, finally add the mushrooms. Cooking them longer would turn them into unrecognizable mush.

7-Taste. Moan with pleasure. Add more salt if desired. Place the coq au vin in a pretty dish. Surround it with potatoes. Pour in the sauce (with mushrooms and pancetta) and sprinkle with finely chopped fresh parley right before serving.

Aubergines au Parmesan

(Eggplant Parmesan)

... Sitting across from Johnny over gooey Eggplant Parmigiana, Annie was as heartbroken as she appeared nonchalant.

Johnny poured the wine into her glass and handed it to her, waited for her to take a sip.

"So?" he said, a half smile on his lips, "you want to get married?"

She swallowed the wine and coughed, "Do you mean in general? I guess one day, with the right man, at the right time."

"No, not in general. I mean the two of us. This week."

A peek at mail boxes and a private garden in Paris

Aubergines au Parmesan -- Eggplant Parmesan

Here is a leaner variation of this recipe: lightly brush olive oil on the eggplant slices (skip the flour) and place the slices in an oven, a barbecue or even a panini maker. You will not obtain the marvelous taste and texture of the fried eggplant, but this is a good alternative for obvious (but depressing) reasons.

Aubergines au Parmesan -- Eggplant Parmesan

Ingredients for four to six servings

2- 28 oz can crushed tomatoes

2 large unpeeled eggplants sliced ½ inch thick. Choose glossy eggplants without exterior blemishes (those can indicate a bad, bad eggplant)

1 cup chopped fresh parsley

½ cup chopped fresh basil

1 tbsp olive oil

1 cup canola oil (perhaps more)

1 cup all-purpose flour

2 cloves of garlic

8 to 10 oz mozzarella, either fresh, thinly sliced or shredded

3 oz grated Parmesan cheese

Salt and pepper to taste (careful as the crushed tomatoes might already contain enough salt)

Directions

1-Heat the oil in a deep casserole. When the oil is hot but not smoking add the chopped parsley and crushed garlic and stir. Being careful it doesn't burn, quickly add both cans of tomatoes and stir. Reduce the heat and simmer uncovered so that the sauce reduces. You want a sauce that is moist but not runny, thick but not pasty. Let it bubble up gently on the stove while you prepare the rest of the recipe.

2-In a plate sprinkle flour on both sides of the eggplant. Some people sprinkle the eggplant slices with salt and let it sweat. I've never had the patience. Reserve the eggplant slices and toss the remaining flour. Heat the canola oil. When it is very hot but not smoking, add a layer of eggplant. Cook for 2 to 3 minutes, flip and cook the other side. The goal is not to cook the eggplant slice but to grill its sides. Place the semi-cooked eggplant slices on 2 sheets of paper towel and repeat with the rest of the eggplant slices. Now here comes the moment of truth: it will take much more oil than I was comfortable revealing, but by now you're in too deep and can't turn back.

3- Take a look at the sauce. Does it look sexy yet? Any last minute adjustment? If it reduced too much, cover, lower the heat, add water, or all of the above. If it's too liquid, drain some of the liquid out, uncover, turn up the heat, or all of the above (don't turn on the heat and walk away as the sauce will burn and your life will be ruined.) Five minutes before assembling add the basil and stir. I personally like basil that was not overcooked.Add pepper and salt to taste.

4- Now comes the fun part. Decide if you're going for the family style vibe or the fancy-shmancy look and choose either a pretty oven-proof dish (about 9 x 9), or ramekins for individual portions. For extra garlic taste and an evening of fragrant garlic kisses, rub a peeled garlic clove on the bottom and sides of the dish.

5- Cover the bottom of the dish with sauce. Place one layer of eggplant slices. Sprinkle the eggplant with a generous amount of Parmesan cheese while loudly singing O Sole Mio. Add layers of eggplant and grated Parmesan until you've used it all. Top with layer of fresh mozzarella. Cover with the remainder of the sauce.

6- Wait for your guests to arrive before this last step. When they do, place the dish(es) in the oven at 350 °F for 30 to 40 minutes or until the sauce is bubbly and the cheese melts. Before serving add a few leaves or parsley or basil as a garnish.

7- Serve with pasta, garlic bread, Caesar salad, or anything vaguely Italian you can think of.

Couscous Marocain

(Moroccan Couscous)

...Althea recognized couscous. Annie had served it once and she had not dared taste it at the time. But today she would. She would wait in line and be served steaming couscous, and maybe one of the thin spicy sausages.

But before Althea could get closer to the food stands the crowd carried her away, toward an area of vibrant color: rugs, gold, jewels, beads, and Indian fabrics, piles of it, caressed by a woman in a sari so green and vivid it was fluorescent. The woman's wrinkled hands like leather on silk.

Everywhere, there were children with cotton candy in their hands darting around their mothers like flashes of light."

Jardin du Luxembourg, a candy shack très rétro.

Couscous Marocain -- Moroccan Couscous

Couscous Marocain -- Moroccan Couscous

Ingredients for four to six servings

¼ cup canola oil

1tbsp butter

2 pounds chicken, lamb, or beef (or just go nuts and use all three.)

5 large peeled carrots (cut into 1 inch chunks)

4 unpeeled zucchini (ends removed, cut into 1 inch cubes)

2 peeled turnips (chose small ones, and if possible spring turnips. Large old turnips can be bitter and stringy, yuck.)

3 large tomatoes (finely chopped) or one 14-oz can crushed tomatoes

1 large onion, chopped

1 cup fresh cilantro leaves (remove stems)

1 tsp salt

1 tbsp ginger powder

2 tbsp cumin powder

½ tsp pepper

¼ tsp red pepper flakes

5 or 6 saffron threads

3 cups dry couscous grains (with ¼ tsp salt when cooking)

Optional: Spicy Merguez sausages can be cooked separately and placed them on top of the completed dish.

Directions

1- In a 4 to 6 quart pan (Dutch oven or French oven style), heat the oil and butter until the butter starts sizzling, then add all the meat and brown on all sides. (You might have to do this in several batches.)

2- Add the finely chopped onion and stir until it is slightly translucent.

3- Add all the spices and the salt, cook for 3 minutes while stirring. Hmmm...is it me or is your kitchen beginning to smell deliciously North African?

4- Add fresh cilantro and tomatoes and continue to cook for 3 minutes while stirring.

5- Add the carrots.

6- Add just enough water to cover the meat and vegetables and bring to a boil. Lower the temperature and cover so that the stew simmers gently for one hour.

7- Add turnips and cook for 15 more minutes.

8- Add unpeeled zucchini and cook for 15 more minutes.

9- 15 minutes before serving, bring 4 cups of salted water to a boil. As soon as the water boils, turn off the heat and add the dry couscous. Stir, cover tightly with plastic wrap so that no water evaporates. (The 'right' way to cook couscous is to steam it. I'm personally unable to taste the difference.) It should take about five to seven minutes.

10- Separate the cooked couscous with a fork, then place it in a mound in the center of a large platter.

11- Strain the meat and vegetables through a fine sieve, saving the liquid. Delicately place the vegetable and meat all around the couscous grains. Serve the liquid in a separate dish (such as tureen).

12- Tell your guests that they must help themselves from the dish with their bare right hand (never the left!), 'because that's how you're supposed to eat couscous', and enjoy the mortified look on their faces. Once you've had your fun, hand them forks and knives.

Croque Monsieur

...Inside the café, the noise level was deafening, what with the espresso machines expelling their steam and waiters calling orders and the clanking of dishes and utensils. The counter was so crowded that Lucas had to sip his espresso with his shoulders perpendicular to it. Apparently, no one seemed ready to venture out of the groggy and womb-like atmosphere of the two-hour lunch break. People actually liked being here, even though the air was saturated with the smell of cigarettes and Plat du Jour, and steam from humidity and human heat clouded the windows. A tall man with a lifetime of practice at carving himself a spot in busy Parisian cafés, Lucas didn't usually resent the invasion of his personal space, but today, it was insufferable. His mood was not improved by the spectacle of Jared, unshaven, unwashed, and devouring his second greasy Croque-Monsieur with his left arm and shoulder literally glued to him.

The lines under the Eiffel Tower

Croque Monsieur

A croque monsieur is so much more than a grilled cheese sandwich. In France it is ubiquitous and the essence of a quick meal in a French cafés. The croque monsieur can be held responsible for thickening its share of Parisian waistlines.

Croque Monsieur

Ingredients for four croque monsieurs

8 slices of white bread cut not too thin (the traditional shape in cafés and restaurant is square, but does it really matter?)

4 slices of plain ham (not smoked or shaved too thin) sliced not too thin

8 oz grated Gruyere cheese

3 oz butter

1/2 cup flour

3 cups milk

A pinch of nutmeg

Pepper and salt to taste

Directions

Taste ham and Gruyere cheese. The amount of salt added to your béchamel will depend on how salty they are.

1- Melt butter in a medium pan.

2-Add flour and stir until absorbed. Do not let it brown.

3-Little by little add all the cold milk while stirring.

4- Stir for about 15 minutes (if you start with warm milk it might take less time.) Continue until thick enough that it will not run when placed on top of the bread.

5- Add salt, pepper, and nutmeg to taste.

6-Toast the bread lightly. Butter lightly.

7- Place a slice of ham neatly on four of the slices of bread.

8- Place no more than a tablespoon béchamel on the ham and spread it around.

9- Divide the grated gruyere in two. Spread half evenly on top of the ham.

10- Place the second toasted bread slice on the grated cheese.

11- Pour the remaining béchamel over each sandwich.

12- Cover each with the remaining grated cheese.

13- Place briefly under the broiler until the cheese is melted and golden. Careful --Gruyere burns quickly.

Serve with a garden salad, something cold, crisp and guilt-free to balance out ultra rich sandwiches.

Endives au Jambon

(Endive in ham and béchamel sauce)

...The last thing Annie wanted to deal with was what Lola called a cooking lesson and what she called misery. Lola had no instinct, no natural inclination when it came to cooking. But already, Lola was following her. "Why don't you sit on the couch and relax with the kids. I'll make dinner," she told Lola. The answer was no, unfortunately. In the kitchen, Annie began to work on her endives au jambon, *washing the endives, arranging slices of ham, grating Gruyère and preparing the béchamel sauce. Lola was in charge of the vinaigrette, a simple enough task she had instructed her on several times. Lola scratched her head before the salt and pepper grinders and the jars of vinegar, olive oil, and mustard "When do you plan on calling Mark?" Annie asked, that question often resulting in Lola running away and giving her some freedom.*

"I, well, not, I didn't, I mean, not yet. So it's vinegar first?..."

A Montparnasse stroll

Endives au Jambon -- endive in ham and béchamel sauce

What do four French girls eat when they gather at home for a girls' night in? I always ask my friend Isabelle if she would bring her wonderful Endives au Jambon. *You could not make me eat raw endives (so bitter!) but somehow, in this recipe, they are transformed into something fabulous.*

This is not the kind of meal served in French restaurants, but you will find it on people's kitchen tables throughout France. This is French comfort food at its most basic and pleasurable.

Endive in ham and béchamel sauce

Ingredients for four (8 servings)

8 medium/large heads of white endive

1 large pot of unsalted water

8 slices of plain ham (not too thin), not flavored or smoked.

8 oz grated Gruyere cheese

3 oz butter

3/4 cup flour

4 cups milk

1 pinch of nutmeg

pepper and salt to taste

Directions

1- Trim the bottom of each endive. If there are blemishes you can remove outer leaves, if not leave as is and rinse.

2- Boil the water. Add the endive and cook on medium boil until you can easily pierce them with a knife. Drain.

3- Butter an ovenproof dish pretty enough to bring to the table (about 9 x 12).

4- Roll a slice of ham neatly around each cooked head of

endive and place in the center of the buttered dish.

5-Time to make a béchamel sauce. But first taste your ham and your cheese. The amount of salt you add to the béchamel will depend on how salty they are.

6- Melt butter in a medium sauce pan.

7-Add flour and stir until absorbed. Do not let it brown.

8-Little by little add all the cold milk while stirring.

9- Stir for a while, about 15 to 20 minutes (if you start with warm milk it will take less time).

10- Add salt, pepper, and a hint of nutmeg to taste.

11- When it has achieved the consistency of pudding, pour the béchamel on top of the ham-wrapped endive.

12- Top with all the grated cheese.

13- Place in a hot oven for up to 30 minutes, until the cheese has obtained a nice golden color. You can place it briefly under the broiler to achieve this, but beware, Swiss cheese burns quickly.

Gigot de Sept Heures

(Lamb Mechoui)

...Annie had been cooking for two days. A méchoui, an entire lamb, had been roasting for hours in the kitchen's giant fireplace, sending its extravagant aroma through the sixteenth arrondissement. She was also making piles of couscous and had baked Tunisian pastries and Moroccan buns with anise seeds.

A famous Colonne Morris, in Paris since 1854.

Gigot de Sept Heures -- Lamb Mechoui

What? You do not own a fire pit large enough to roast an entire lamb? Or perhaps you don't have the heart to run after a baby lamb, catch it and transform it into a kebab version of itself? Consider this alternate version. In France we call this a 'gigot de sept heures'*, or seven hour lamb.*

It really is a wonderfully fragrant way of cooking a leg of lamb. It's effortless to prepare, amazing to eat and fantastic to serve to company because it can be forgotten in the oven where it will do nothing but become ever more delicious by the minute.

Lamb Mechoui

Ingredients for six to eight servings,

depending on the size of the leg of lamb

1 large leg of lamb with bone in

5 peeled shallots

10 unpeeled cloves of garlic

Olive oil

1 tsp coriander seeds

Salt, pepper

1 teaspoon red paper flakes to add some kick

Optional: Root vegetable medley, peeled baby turnips, carrots, baby beets, peeled (I kept the skins on for the picture to achieve a more rustic look)

Directions

I wish I owned a Le Creuset French cast iron pan but never wanted one badly enough to splurge. Mine is a cheap imitation and works perfectly well. All you really need is an ovenproof casserole with a tight lid. The size of the leg of lamb will dictate the size of the pan. If you're cooking for a crowd you can use any pan you would use to cook a turkey and cover the dish tightly with heavy-duty tin foil before placing it in the oven. Because my lid is not tight (sounds like I'm making a comment about myself here) I make a simple dough using 2 cups of flour and a bit of water and I seal it all around the lid, making it airtight. When the time comes to serve I place the dish on the table and break it at the table, which is pretty much awesome. The dough will look like bread but after baking for hours it will be hard as rock and inedible. You might need one of those cute girly hammers to break it.

1-Heat the olive oil, then add the leg of lamb, turning it so that it browns on all sides.

2-Add the peeled, quartered shallots and the coriander seeds.

3-Add the unpeeled cloves of garlic.

4-Add salt and pepper to taste.

5-Cover the pan, place it in the oven at a temperature of 300° F degrees (150°C).

6- Cook for 3 hours at that temperature.

7- Lower the heat to 250° C and cook for another 2 to 4 hours. As long as the lid is sealed tight there will be no loss of juice and the lamb will not get dry, it will only get more delicious. If you feel your lid is not tight (hee hee) add broth or water mid-way though cooking. This is the point when I add braised root vegetables to the pot and make my dough seal. Cook an additional 2 to 4 hours as before.

8- Serve. I like to place the dish on the center of the table, family style. After showing off by breaking the dough, I give each person a few cloves of garlic. Because the skin was not removed the garlic cloves have kept their shape as they cooked in the lamb's juices. On the plate they become miniature containers of garlic jam. Divine!

9- If you did not add root vegetables to the pot, in keeping with the North African theme, you can serve this lamb '*méchoui*' with a vegetable couscous or a refreshing *taboulé*.

Lasagnes Françaises

(French Style Lasagna)

..."How did this materialize?" Lucas cried out in delight an hour later when Annie placed a steaming dish of chicken lasagna and a large Salade Niçoise *in the center of the dining room table.*

"The way to a man's heart is through his stomach," Annie said for Lola's benefit...

La Fontaine's statue in the Ranelagh gardens in the 16th arrondissement

Lasagnes Françaises (French Style Lasagna)

Italians probably have the final say as to what constitutes lasagna, but the French version uses gruyère or fromage de comté. Mozzarella and ricotta are replaced with béchamel. The French version is much more... well, French.

Lasagnes Françaises -- French Style Lasagna

Ingredients for four to six servings

Lasagna

Fresh pasta sheet (see pasta recipe) or 1 box of lasagna pasta preferably the kind that does not require pre-cooking

1 large onion

1 tbsp olive oil

1 clove of garlic

2-28 oz cans crushed tomatoes

2 tsp dried or fresh oregano and/or basil

1 lb ground beef, chicken and/or turkey

1 cup grated strong cheese such as Gruyère, but you might prefer Romano, Parmesan or whatever is on hand

Salt and pepper

Béchamel sauce

2 tbsp. unsalted butter

2 tbsp flour

2 cups low fat milk

1 dash nutmeg to taste

Salt and pepper to taste

Directions

Meat and tomato sauce:

1-Heat the oil in a pan.

2-Add chopped onion and garlic, and sauté for a few minutes until they are golden. Burning them might make them turn bitter.

3- Add the crushed tomatoes. Lower the heat and taste. Add pepper and salt to taste. Add basil and oregano, then simmer for 20 minutes on low heat.

4-In a separate pan, sauté the meat on high heat until it is cooked and all moisture has evaporated.

5- Add to the meat to the tomato sauce.

6- Cook to reduce until the sauce is thick and not runny.

Béchamel sauce

7- In a small pan heat 2 tablespoons butter until it melts without burning or turning brown. Turn off the heat and add two tablespoons flour. Whip it until foamy. Add the cold milk all at once. Replace the pan on the stove and cook on medium heat while whipping until it thickens like custard. Add salt, pepper and nutmeg to taste.

Lasagna assembly

8- This is when little ones can come in and help transform your organized kitchen into a disaster zone. In a rectangular oven proof dish about 9 x 13 or individual *ramekins* (see picture).

a- pour enough béchamel to cover the bottom (about 1/3 of it).

b- add a single layer of lasagna pasta (cut and paste to cover rather than overlap).

c- pour enough tomato and meat sauce to cover the pasta.

d- sprinkle with 1/3 of the shredded cheese.

e- repeat: béchamel layer, pasta layer, meat and tomato sauce layer, shredded cheese layer.

f- add the last layer of pasta, the rest of the béchamel, the rest of the meat and tomato sauce, the rest of the shredded cheese and cook in the oven for about 45 minutes.

9- Serve with a simple salad.

Moelleux au Chocolat

(Moist Chocolate Cake)

...Monsieur François straightened his posture and looked around him as though he was looking for hidden cameras. "C'est une blague?" Is this a joke?

"You see a lot of people every day," Lola said in her best French. "And as a man, what do you think?"

Monsieur François readjusted his sports coat. "I cannot speak for all men, bien sûr..."

Lola smiled encouragingly. "Of course."

He bent down so that his face would be at the same level as theirs and whispered in a seductive breath that smelled of cigarettes and red wine. "I can't be speaking for all men, but, I'd personally be happy to prove Madame l'Américaine, heu--"

"Annie," offered Lola.

"Madame Annie, can count on me to be her... Chevalier Servant. It would be a pleasure. As long as ma femme is left out of all this, of course." He stood up, caressed his mustache, and declared with loud panache as he walked off, "Two Moelleux au Chocolat, Gérard, on the house."

Annie and Lola had to duck under the table to hide their laughter.

Moelleux au Chocolat (Moist Chocolate Cake)

Note: Few restaurants in France would dare to have a dessert menu lacking crème brûlée or moelleux au chocolat. 'Moelleux' means moist, bordering on gooey.

I can prepare this recipe while blindfolded with both hands tied behind my back. Ten minutes to prepare, under 20 minutes to bake and it can be served piping hot from the oven. I have personally never met a more cook-friendly chocolate cake, or one that is more popular.

Moelleux au Chocolat -- Moist Chocolate Cake

Ingredients for a 9 inch round cake

1 cup semi-sweet chocolate chips

1 stick unsalted butter

2 large eggs

1 tsp real vanilla extract

¼ tsp salt

½ cup granulated sugar

½ cup light brown sugar

½ cup ground raw almonds (roasted almonds would change the taste 100%. The taste of almond is barely noticeable in this recipe but it takes the place of flour to give the cake its fabulous consistency)

½ cup corn starch or preferably potato starch. You can find potato starch in the Jewish cooking section of supermarkets, especially around Passover. I usually buy many boxes at that time because I'm never sure when I'll find it again.

Directions

1-Place the stick of butter and the chocolate chips in a microwave-proof dish and cook on high for exactly one minute. Stir until smooth. You might need to heat a few more seconds and re-stir if not smooth.

2- Preheat_oven to 350°F.

3- In a medium bowl, beat eggs, then add granulated and brown sugar. Stir until well mixed. Add salt and vanilla.

4- Add the butter and chocolate mixture to the egg and sugar mixture. Beat until homogenous. Add ground raw almond and corn or potato starch. Stir well.

5- Grease a 9-inch round cake pan. Line the bottom with parchment paper and smear a bit of butter on the paper.

6- Pour the batter into the prepared cake pan.

7- Place in the oven. After 25 minutes, insert a blade into the center of the cake. It should come out neither gooey (undercooked, and entirely delicious but my enthusiasm for liquid centers is tempered by my fear of salmonella) nor clean (dry as a bone) but somewhere in between. Serve at room temperature or slightly warm, with vanilla ice cream for full effect.

Mousse au Chocolat

(Chocolate Mousse)

... "There is an endive and beet salad, and for dessert, a mousse au chocolat," she added, speaking to no one in particular, "Jared, he is too independent to be having dinner with us every night, but tonight, he is bestowing on us the honor of his company."

Lucas was giving the shorthaired woman a wine tasting lesson, twirling her glass by putting his hand over hers; neither of them paid attention to Annie. "What did you say her name was?" Jared asked Annie in a low voice so that the other two wouldn't hear.

"Oh, yeah, Casanova is waking up? Lola is married with children and Lucas has obviously claimed her for himself from the moment she landed here." Annie stepped toward the refrigerator angrily.

Of course he wasn't asking about that woman. "Stop calling me Casanova and Don Juan. D'accord?" he said.

"Whatever you say, Romeo!"

Mousse au Chocolat (Chocolate Mousse)

Note: there is no added sugar in this mousse, so you are relying on the chocolate to sweeten the recipe. If you use unsweetened chocolate, your guests might look at you cross-eyed.

Also, at the risk of being a party pooper, if you have a weakened immune system, are pregnant, are a child, an older person, or suffer from mild to severe hypochondria, do not eat raw eggs.

Mousse au Chocolat -- Chocolate Mousse

Ingredients for four to six servings

3 eggs of irreproachable freshness and lineage

1 cup semi-sweet chocolate chips

1 tsp vanilla extract

pinch of salt

Directions

1-Separate egg yolks from the whites. Place whites in a large bowl or in the bowl of your electric mixer. Make sure the bowl is very clean and at a temperature close to the eggs'. Now, I've never failed to beat egg whites to the desired stiffness but there seems to be people who have. The trick is to keep the bowl at a temperature close to the eggs, make sure that none of the yolk gets into the white, and that the bowl is clean and dry. Then add elbow grease.

2- Melt the chocolate with a tablespoon of water in a glass dish in the microwave (or use the double boiler method if you prefer cleaning a lot of extra pans.)

3- Add the vanilla and egg yolks to the melted chocolate one by one and stir rapidly to incorporate. Add one yolk at a time so that they won't cook in the heat of the chocolate.

4- While the chocolate mixture cools, beat the egg whites until they are firm enough that a spoon can stand when placed in the center of the bowl. Halfway through beating the eggs add the salt.

5- Add the beaten egg whites to the egg yolks and chocolate mixture. Then ever so gently, and in a scooping and folding motion, fold the chocolate mixture and the egg whites together with a spatula, careful not to rush which would break the precious bubbles that make this a mousse.

6- When the mix is homogeneous, divide into 4 pretty bowls and refrigerate for 1 to 2 hours. Serve with berries and maybe a dash of whipped cream.

Paella aux Fruits de Mer

(Seafood Paella)

..."Althea, how come you're this skinny?" Annie asked. The sentence was no sooner out of her mouth that Lola was giving her a look and shaking her head in an emphatic no.

"I'm not exactly skinny," Althea responded as she peeled a potato in one long, graceful ribbon. "There are areas that have cellulite on them," she continued in a flat voice. "Like my inner thighs."

Annie worked on her paella, coating the clams and shrimps evenly with juice with one hand while picking uncontrollably at the baguette with the other. "Your inner what?"

Althea wore jeans that were probably the equivalent of a size zero, yet were baggy on her. She stood from her chair and grabbed the inside of her pant leg. "Here."

Annie laughed, "Well, if you're not skinny, then I'm obese."

Althea considered that information. "I guess you're...curvaceous," she said with an oh-so-subtle grimace of disgust.

"Gee, thanks! I do like to think of myself as curvaceous. Curvaceous is good in my book," Annie said, but her feelings were hurt.

Paella aux Fruits de Mer -- Seafood Paella

The French adore Spanish Paella. I took a picture of this fantastic giant paella and stew at the Trouville *outdoor market (in the Normandy region, right on the pier). Can you imagine the scent of Paella and roasted chicken wafting through the outdoor market? Can you imagine eating the warm Paella at a* pique-nique sur la plage*?*

Paella aux Fruits de Mer -- Seafood Paella

Ingredients for six to eight servings

2 tbsp canola or safflower oil

2 quarts fish stock (or make from scratch using 1 whole crab, salt, and pepper), or chicken broth

1 lb mussels and clams (must be tightly closed)

6 chicken thighs

2 chorizos (or milder sausage if you prefer)

¾ lb raw shrimp

½ lb chopped calamari

2 tbsp butter

2 small onions, chopped

3 cloves of garlic, chopped

2 sweet red peppers, diced

4 small zucchini, diced

3 tomatoes in season or

1-28 oz can whole tomatoes

1lb short grain rice such as Arborio. Avoid Asian rice or the kind of rice that becomes creamy such as risotto.

1large pinch saffron threads

2 cups fresh or frozen peas

Salt and pepper

Directions

You will need two pans: one to cook and the other to hold the ingredients that have already been cooked. Once an ingredient is cooked, keep it warm in a 200° oven: enough to keep warm but not hot enough to dry or overcook.

1-Cut the chorizo into ½ inch thick slices. Dice the red peppers and remove all seeds. Dice the tomatoes if they are fresh. Peel and finely chop garlic and onion. Chop the calamari into ½ inch bits.

2-Heat the vegetable oil in a wide skillet. Sauté the chorizo on all sides. Add the chicken and sauté on all sides. Add 2 cups of broth and cover. Cook for 20 minutes on medium heat. Add a bit of broth and/or lower the heat as needed so that it won't burn. Set aside the chorizo and chicken and keep warm. Make sure all the juices remain in the skillet.

3-In the same pan, sauté the shrimp in the juices. After 2 minutes, add 1 cup of broth. Cover and cook for about 6 minutes. Reserve the shrimp and keep warm in 200° F oven. Let all the juices evaporate in the pan but don't let it burn.

4-In the same pan, add a bit of oil and sauté the calamari. Reserve and keep warm. Let all the juices evaporate again.

5-In the same pan, add a bit of oil and sauté the diced onions until translucent. Add the red peppers and stir. Add garlic and stir. Now add the canned (no need to drain) or fresh chopped tomatoes, and stir for 5 minutes.

6-Add the rice to pan and stir well, coating the rice with the tomato sauce. Add the amount of broth recommended on the rice package. Add saffron threads. After the initial boil, lower the heat to medium and cover for 20 minutes or until the stock has been absorbed. Halfway though this process, decide if your rice is yellow enough and, if needed, add saffron to darken it to a nice sunflower gold.

7- Before the rice is cooked all the way, add chopped zucchini and peas and cook until the rice is still firm but not crunchy. If the stock is absorbed but the rice is still crunchy, add stock, one cup at a time, cover, and continue to cook until the rice is tender. Taste and add salt if needed. (If you run out of stock, which you might have already, don't panic. Water will do at this point since the flavor has been built.)

8-While the rice finishes cooking, bring two cups of fish/chicken stock to a boil in a separate pan. Drop the clams and mussels into the pot. Cover and cook for ten minutes. Discard any clams or mussels that did not open. You can add the leftover liquid to the cooking rice.

9-Once the rice is cooked, place it in a mound in a wide, shallow dish. Retrieve all the cooked ingredients from the oven where they have been kept warm. Place the chicken, chorizo and shrimp around the rice. Top with mussels and clams.

10- Mix and serve at the table in front of your guests.

Accompany with white wine, cold beer, a simple green salad and a faux Spanish accent.

Pâtes à la Carbonara

(Pasta Carbonara)

..."I don't think it's Lucas that Althea is trying to avoid," Annie told Lola. "I think it's my food."

"What do you mean?"

"Yesterday Althea said she would be with us at the table as long as she could eat her own food. She said my cooking doesn't agree with her. Weird, but fine with me. Better than having her bring a heaping plate of Linguini a la Carbonara to her room and shoving it down the toilet behind my back like she did the other day."

"How do you know she did that?" Lola seemed shocked.

"The pancetta bits refused to be flushed. I guess their high fat content brought them back to the surface of the john's water, an interesting piece of trivia. I told Althea that I noticed her tossing food down the toilet, that I wasn't a complete numskull."

Lola thought for a moment. "Do you mean she tossed it before or after *eating it?" she asked.*

Summer evening on the Quais de Seine

Pâtes à la Carbonara -- Pasta Carbonara

Rather than add cheese to this high calorie recipe, I prefer to serve shaved Parmesan on the side. This dish is easy to make and represents comfort food in its purest form. What it is not, however, is kosher, vegan, nondairy or gluten-free. It will help clog your arteries and some people should not eat it as it contains raw eggs. What's not to love!

Pâtes à la Carbonara -- Pasta Carbonara

Ingredients for four servings

1 cup diced pancetta. (The traditional recipe calls for French *lardons* but here in the U.S. I substitute with Pancetta, which you can find already cut at Trader Joe's or cut to order at good grocery stores and butchers)

1 large peeled shallot, finely chopped

2 incredibly fresh egg (yolks only)

1/2 cup heavy cream

1/2 cup Parmesan cheese (preferably shaved)

1/3 cup finely chopped fresh chives or parsley (optional)

Salt and black pepper

Freshly made or store bought pasta such as linguini or spaghetti

Directions

1-Place the diced pancetta in a pan and cook on medium heat until golden.

2- Lower the heat and add the chopped shallot. Stir and cook until the shallot bits are translucent, not golden.

3- Add cream and black pepper; stir well. Taste the cream. Usually the pancetta contains enough salt for this dish but you can add salt to taste. Because the pasta cooks in salted water and you will be adding Parmesan cheese, the sauce can become overly salty, so keep a light touch.

4- Keep sauce warm on extremely low heat (so that the cream does not separate) until ready to serve.

5- Cook your favorite pasta (or better yet, make fresh pasta from scratch... but that's my next book) in a large pot of salted water until al dente according to the package's direction. Drain.

6- At the table, pour the Carbonara sauce on the pasta. Right before stirring add the two egg yolks, drizzle with the herbs. Stir and serve. Let everyone add Parmesan to taste.

7- A crisp green salad with a light vinaigrette and a glass of chardonnay will accompany your *pâtes à la carbonara* very well.

Poisson en Croûte de Sel

(Salt Encrusted whole Fish)

Crust! Salt Encrusted Sea Bass. The recipe called for one kilo of coarse sea salt from the Guérande region — the use of lowly table salt apparently a punishable offense in French cookbooks. The recipe looked impossibly difficult to prepare or shop for. Perfect. She grabbed the Pokémon calculator and punched in numbers. Ten years after moving to France, she still converted recipes from French to English, grammes to ounces, and centilitres to cups.

It's not that she could not learn, it's that she had her own insubordinate way of doing things. Food residues on the calculator cracked and popped, and she took satisfaction in the revelation that her calculator too was en croûte.

A Péniche at sunset

Poisson en Croûte de Sel (Salt Encrusted whole Fish)

Note: I had never made this recipe until I wrote this book. I wanted to include it but I think that at the time I wrote the novel I chose this recipe to symbolize a woman who is not afraid to take risks in the kitchen. Meanwhile, I myself had never taken that risk. I did not quite believe you could use this much salt and not ruin the fish. Now I realize how wrong I was to use this recipe to represent culinary audacity. This is the easiest recipe to make, and the fish comes out delicate, moist, and perfectly balanced, with just the right amount of saltiness.

Poisson Croûte de Sel -- Salt Encrusted whole Fish

Ingredients for four to six depending on size of fish

Fish

1 2 to 3 lb. whole fish such as Sea Bass, White Fish, Blue Fish, or Salmon. The fish must be gutted but with the head and head still attached and the skin and scales on.

1 lb coarse salt for every 2 lb fish. The coarser the salt the better (which is why Guérande salt is better, but it's too expensive in the U.S.) Fine salt risks seeping through the skin of the fish, so avoid it.

2 egg whites

½ cup water

A large baking sheet (long enough to accommodate the fish sideways),lined with parchment paper for easy clean up

Sauce beurre blanc

1 stick of butter cut into cubes and at room temperature (extremely soft but not melted)

1 cup white wine

½ cup peeled and thinly minced shallots

Directions

1- Although serving a whole fish, skin, head and all can seem counterintuitive, the skin prevents the salt from seeping into the flesh of the fish, and the scales make it easier for the skin to come off with salt crust. The head and tail… just look cool. If the fish has already been scaled it's fine. The salt crust will come off first and the skin will need to be removed separately.

But do NOT attempt a salt crust on skinless fish. I tested it for you and the result is inedible.

2- Pat the fish dry. If you wish you can stuff the cavity of the fish with a few slices of lemon, a sprig or two of dill, or other fresh herbs such as parsley, rosemary, or sage. I usually prefer not to stuff the cavity of fish to obtain a purer flavor.

3- in a large bowl, whisk together the salt, beaten egg whites, and about 1/3 cup water. The consistency should be that of the kind of coarse wet sand you can make sand castles with; easy to shape. If you want you can add a bit more water but not enough to dissolve the salt.

4- Place enough salt mixture on the baking sheet to cover the length of the fish minus the head and tail. Pack it tightly to about ¼ in. thick.

5- Place the fish on top of the salt bed.

6- Make sure the cavity of the fish does not get filled with salt as you mound salt around the fish. Then cover the fish with the remainder of the salt. Pack the salt on and around the fish in a coat about ¼ in. thick. Leave the tail and head out of the salt so people can recognize the fish as it comes out.

7- Place the tray in a 400°F oven. Cooking time will depend on the size of your fish. If you do not have a good *pifometre,* (French slang culinary instinct), it's best to insert a meat thermometer in the thickest part of the fish (not through the cavity.) The fish is cooked when the thermometer indicates between 135°F. and 160°F. It usually takes 30 to 40 minutes.

8- While the fish cooks, prepare your *beurre blanc*. A *beurre blanc* (you do not pronounce the c in blanc) is a fabulous invention, a simple buttery sauce that complements fish beautifully. It can be flavored with lemon zest, lemon juice, capers, or dill or left as is (my preference for this recipe).

9- In a medium saucepan, pour the wine, and add the finely minced shallots. Cook until most of the liquid has gone, stirring toward the end until all that is left in the pan are the reduced shallots and a kind of thick glaze.

10- Remove from the heat and start adding the softened butter, one small bit at a time, whisking it constantly so that the butter is not melted but emulsified. Continue with the rest of the butter. If it becomes difficult to emulsify the butter, place it on very gentle heat for a moment, then continue away from the heat. Never let it melt.

11- Add salt and pepper to taste.

12- Stain the sauce (optional).

13- When it's time to serve, I suggest you warm up your sauce serving dish by immersing it in hot water for a few minutes.

14- When the fish is cooked the salt crust will be slightly golden in places. Bring the fish on its baking tray to the table where it can be admired, and the crust can be broken in front of your guests, making you look like Mario Batali. The fish can actually stay there for as long as ten minutes before opening. Imagine the suspense! Break the crust by tapping on it a few times with a spoon. Peel the salt crust back. If the skin does not come out with the salt crust, peel it with two spoons (forks would break the skin.) Using the same spoon, remove the fish fillets, pulling them away from the spine first so that the ribs remain attached to the vertebra. Place the fillets on each plate, careful not to leave chunks of salt on the plate.

15-Drizzle delicious beurre blanc over each fillet.

16- Serve with steamed potatoes or pasta and maybe something green such as French string beans.

Potage de Poulet

(Chicken Soup)

...The decision was made and that was that. Annie felt the nausea of someone about to plunge into the void. She got up and turned on the heat under the soup pot. She'd boil it; hopefully bacteria would get the message. She desperately needed to ingest something liquid, thick, warm and salty like amniotic fluid before she could give birth to her action. Her subconscious must have known she should prepare chicken soup for her future nauseated self...

Notre Dame at dusk

Potage de Poulet -- Chicken Soup

I have to laugh at this excerpt from Hidden in Paris. Not so appetizing... But chicken soup as we all know is so much more than food. It a bone fide cure for various ailments. That, and of course red wine.

Potage de Poulet --Chicken Soup

Ingredients for six to eight servings

1 leftover chicken carcass (with some chicken still on) or small whole chicken

8 cups water or more to fill the pot

4 celery stalks

4 large carrots, peeled

4 small turnips, peeled. (Preferably spring turnips, as older ones can be bitter)

1 medium onion

4 small potatoes, peeled

1 chicken bouillon cube (this gives the soup some oomph.)

Salt & pepper to taste

1/2 tsp dried thyme

1 small bay leaf

(optional) Once the soup is made it's nice to add ½ cup very small pasta of your choice, the kind that cooks in a few minutes; alphabet pasta, vermicelli, stars etc. This is also the ideal soup in which to cook Matzo balls. Make Matzo balls according to the package's direction and drop into the slowly bubbling soup, cover and cook for 20 minutes extra.

Directions

1- Chop peeled carrots and celery stalks into very thin slices. Cut peeled turnips and potatoes into large chunks. You can also choose not to chop the vegetables. Just peel and cook whole. The later will make for a different look and experience (see picture).

2- Fill a large pot with water to within 3 inches from the top of the pot. Brandish your chicken carcass as though you're about to throw it across the kitchen.

3- Gleefully dump it and EVERY ingredient in the recipe (but the salt and pepper and pasta/Matzo balls) into the pot. Turn on the stove.

4- Once the water boils turn the heat down, cover, and simmer for one and a half to two hours.

5- Remove the chicken carcass. Be carefully because it will fall apart and you must make sure that no bones are left in the pot. A broken tooth does not make a happy guest. Let the carcass cool, then pick every bit of chicken off the carcass and add the bits back into the pot. Discard the carcass.

6- Bring the soup back to near boiling. Taste. (Be careful not to burn your mouth, blow first! Easier said than done. I've been burning my mouth on chicken soup for 20 years). Now is the time to decide how much salt you want in the soup: I usually add a chicken bouillon cube at that point for added flavor but it also replaces salt. If you do, make sure the bouillon cube is fully dissolved before you taste the soup again. Add salt and pepper as desired.

7- Add pasta if you choose to and boil five more minutes (or you can add Matzo balls in the soup and let them cook, covered, for 20 minutes, then add pasta in the last 5 minutes.)

8- Serve piping hot in a soup tureen or individual soup bowls. Accompany with toasted bread slices. Throw away your decongestant pills -- you won't need them any more.

Poulet à l'Estragon

(Tarragon Chicken)

...Jared mumbled hello and went about the room gathering plates, utensils, bread, and fruit.

Annie exchanged a meaningful glance with Lola, silenced Paul's giggles with a death stare and got up. She didn't miss a beat. She took a ladle and a medium-size serving bowl from the cupboard, scooped out a generous portion of tarragon chicken, and handed it to Jared as though this were the most natural thing in the world. She might be festering with curiosity but she'd be damned if she showed it.

A Haussmannian building in the 16th arrondissement of Paris

Poulet à l'Estragon -- Tarragon Chicken

French tarragon (estragon in French) is an herb present in much of Provençal cooking. It is sometimes difficult to find fresh French tarragon but there is no point in making this recipe with dry tarragon. Once dry, the herb tastes and smells entirely different and, in my humble opinion, has nothing much to offer.

Now that I live in the U.S. I have grown accustomed to using heavy cream rather than crème fraîche because the latter is harder to find.

Poulet à l'Estragon -- Tarragon Chicken

Ingredients for six servings

8 pieces of chicken (regular or boneless and skinless, a leaner version that also is less flavorful.)

1 tbsp canola oil

1 tsp unsalted butter

2 medium shallots, finely chopped

2 cups chicken broth

3 tbsp white wine vinegar or rice vinegar

1 tbsp strong French Dijon mustard

2 cups white wine

1 tsp red pepper flakes

2 tbsp fresh tarragon, chopped or not. Separate from the stems but reserve those.

1/2 cup heavy cream or crème fraîche

Fresh tarragon for garnish

Salt and pepper to taste

Directions

1- In a 4 to 6 quart pan (Dutch oven or French oven style), melt butter and oil until the butter begins to sizzle, then add the pieces of chicken and sauté them to all side until they are golden(you might have to do this in several batches).

2- Once the chicken is golden on all sides, remove from the pan and set aside.

3- Lower the heat. Add the finely chopped shallots and stir for a minute. Do not let the shallots burn.

4- Still on low heat, deglaze your pan, first by adding the vinegar and stirring, then adding the wine and stirring. When all the juices have been deglazed and mixed in, add Dijon mustard and stir, then add chicken stock and place the chicken back into the pan.

5- Add black pepper, red pepper flakes, the tarragon stems and half the tarragon leaves.

6- Cover and cook on medium heat for 20 minutes. Remove the cover, stir, and cook for an additional 10 minutes or more until the sauce has reduced by half (overcooking the chicken is perfectly okay for this recipe.) Taste and add salt and pepper to taste. Some chicken broths are saltier than others; so make sure to taste before adding salt. Cover and cook on low heat. Make sure the sauce doesn't reduce too much. If it becomes too thick add up to 1 cup of water or chicken broth.

7- A few minutes before serving, remove and discard the tarragon stalks. Reheat the dish thoroughly on the stove. Once it is hot add the cream and turn off the heat so that the cream does not separate. Two tablespoons is enough to give the dish a creamy texture. I like a lot of cream.

8-Place your tarragon chicken in a pretty dish, pour the sauce over it and sprinkle with a bit of fresh chopped tarragon.

9- Serve with basmati rice or pasta, red or white wine and string beans, fresh peas when in season, or a green salad.

Poulet Provençal

(Chicken Provencal)

...The place was so lovely, with the sound of crickets, the smell of the Italian cypress, and that sea breeze from the Mediterranean. "There is a retired couple who lives there year-round," Annie said. "They keep up the property, cook, and clean for Lucas and his guests in the summer months. Madame Denis and I hit it off. She taught me everything I know about Provencal cooking."

In truth, Madame Denis had reminded Annie of her own mother and they had both cried when it was time to go...

Cobblestone steps in a 5th arrondissement alley.

Poulet Provençal -- Chicken Provencal

Next to roaming free range in an organic environment, chickens are happiest when prepared à la provençale. I know this for a fact having personally interviewed dozens of chickens.

Poulet Provençal -- Chicken Provencal

Ingredients for 6 to 8 servings

1-28 oz can crushed tomatoes, or 4 large very ripe tomatoes, diced.

10-12 pieces of chicken (With skin and bone is kinder on the wallet and the taste buds. Skinless, boneless is kinder on the waistline)

2 large or 4 small red peppers cleaned, seeded and cut into strips

2 carrots, peeled and cut into thin slices

2 large onions, finely chopped

6 cloves of garlic, peeled and slightly crushed

½ bottle of cheap white wine (or expensive if you're a millionaire)

½ cup chopped fresh parsley

1 bay leaf

½ tsp dried thyme, or a few sprigs of fresh thyme

½ tsp dried or fresh rosemary

¼ cup canola oil

1tbsp white flour (to thicken the sauce)

¼ tsp red pepper flakes, if you like a bit of a kick.

Directions

1- In a large pot, heat half the oil. Add onion and garlic and stir until the onions are translucent. Do not let it burn.

2- Remove the onions from the pot, set aside. Add remaining oil to the pot. Sauté the chicken until is it golden on all sides.

3- Sprinkle the flour over the chicken and stir.

4- Add the white wine, crushed tomatoes, red pepper flakes, parsley, thyme, rosemary, and bay leaf. Return the cooked onions to the pot. Add water if needed so that all the chicken is covered in liquid. Bring to a boil.

5- Meanwhile steam (or microwave covered for 5 minutes) the strips of red pepper and the carrots. This will soften and precook the vegetables just enough.

6- Once the liquid in the chicken pot has boiled, reduce heat to a simmer, add the cooked red peppers and carrots, cover, and cook at least one hour.

7- Taste, add salt if necessary, and serve over white rice.

Ragout de la Mer

(Fish Stew)

..."Look who's back!" Annie exclaimed. "God's gift to mankind! Where have you been?"

Jared made an evasive hand gesture. "Is it all right with you if I bring dinner to my room?"

Annie gave Jared a dirty look, shrugged and took a large plate from the cabinet. Lucas watched her fill the plate with pasta, pour over it a heaping serving of fish stew that overflowed with mussels, shrimp, and red sauce, and top it with a sprig of parsley. She handed the plate to Jared. "You want something else? Dessert? Bread?"

"Non, c'est parfait," he said. He thanked her and left the kitchen like a robber carrying his loot, the aroma of fish, white wine, and tomatoes following him up the dark stairs.

"The hell with these people," Annie said.

The outdoor market in Trouville

Ragout de la Mer -- Fish Stew

You can add crab to this recipe for instant glamor. You can buy cooked crabmeat and warm it up by setting it on top of the clams and mussels while they cook. One thing I always do at the seafood counter (and the reason they eye me with suspicion at Whole Foods) is ask to smell the shellfish. It should smell like the ocean, nothing more. Sure I seem odd, but rather that than bring home nasty-smelling crab.

Ragout de la Mer -- Fish Stew

Ingredients for four to six servings

Your choice of 4 filets of monkfish, sole, tilapia, whitefish and/or salmon

½ lb mussels tightly shut

½ lb small clams tightly shut

½ lb peeled raw shrimp

2 tbsp butter

3 peeled, chopped shallots

¼ bottle cheap white wine

1 small glass of cognac (optional)

1-28 oz can crushed tomatoes or 6 diced fresh ripe tomatoes

1 peeled clove of garlic, crushed or minced

2 tbsp flour

1/2 pint heavy cream, or 3 tbsp crème fraîche

Salt and pepper

¼ tsp rosemary (dry or fresh)

½ tsp thyme (dry or fresh)

Red pepper flakes (to give it a kick)

Directions

1-Melt the butter in a large skillet (one with a lid). Before it gets too hot add the shallots. Stir over very low heat as you do not want the shallots to burn (they turn bitter). When the shallots are a bit translucent, add the flour and stir. Before the flour changes color, add the cognac and/or wine. Stir and bring to a gentle boil. Add one and a half cups of water.

2-Add the peeled shrimp and tightly shut mussels and clams to the pot and close the lid. Steam for 7 minutes. The mussels and clams will release their liquid into the sauce and build its flavor, which is why you want to steam there rather than in a separate pot. Remove shrimp, mussels and clams from the pot. Any that did not open must be discarded. Keep warm in a dish by covering with aluminum foil.

3- Add tomatoes, pepper flakes, and crushed clove of garlic to the juices inside the pot. Gently boil sauce for ten minutes. Add thyme and rosemary

4-Place all your pieces of fish delicately on top of the sauce, cover and simmer until the fish is cooked (check by inserting a the blade of a knife and making sure the center isn't gooey or translucent).

5-Delicately remove the fish and place it on the dish that contains the mussels and shrimp. Keep warm for a few minutes.

6-Add the heavy cream to the sauce. Add salt and pepper to taste. Stir and reduce for 2 minutes.

7- Pour the sauce in a wide low serving dish. Place the fish on top of the sauce and arrange the shrimp, mussels and clams around it. Add cooked crab meat, or crab legs on top if you choose.

8- Serve piping hot with steamed, peeled potatoes, rice or pasta.

Salade Niçoise

(South of France Salad)

...Annie did feel a touch of pride at her planning skills. She had prepared the lasagna and washed the ingredients of the Salade Niçoise the day before, then warmed up one dish and tossed the other with homemade vinaigrette, and a meal was ready to eat within a half hour of her mysterious guests arriving from the airport....

A potted garden in a Parisian alley

Salade Niçoise --South of France Salad

Salade Niçoise is another way to say 'Summer' in France. A popular serving option in the South of France especially the beach towns of Nice and Cannes, is what is known as the "Pan Bagnat." Toss the salad with the vinaigrette and serve it inside individual round French bread loaves like a sandwich (Ciabatta bread also works well). Eat on the beach wearing only a bikini bottom and a straw hat.

Salade Niçoise --South of France Salad

Ingredients for four to six servings

Salad

One large head romaine or butter lettuce

4 medium size potatoes

2 large or 4 small ripe tomatoes

4 eggs

½ pound green beans

1 English cucumber (if using regular cucumber, remove seeds)

1 sweet red pepper

1-6 oz can tuna (must be canned or it's not Niçoise. It doesn't matter if it's in oil or water)

10 small black olives, pitted

1 can flat anchovy fillets

Vinaigrette

1/2 cup salad oil (canola, safflower but avoid olive oil for this unless it tastes really mild)

3 tbsp red wine vinegar

1 tbsp strong plain French mustard (Trader Joe's, Maille)

Salt, pepper

Directions

1-Place eggs in enough cold water to cover them. Bring to a slow boil. Cook for 7 minutes. Let the eggs cool for a few minutes. Remove the shells under running water. Cut the shelled eggs into halves or quarters.

2- Use the same process for potatoes, only this time you can add salt to the water. Cook the potatoes in salted water for about 20 minutes or just until a knife can easily pierce them. If you overcook, the potatoes might fall apart into mush. Remove skin under running water after cooking (or peel beforehand). Cut into chunks about the size of the quartered eggs.

3- Trim the green beans, cut them in 1 inch pieces, and steam until soft (5 minutes). The less you cook them the firmer,greener, and prettier they will be, (you don't want limp string beans in your Niçoise) but don't undercook either.

4- Cut tomatoes into quarters.

5- Remove the red peppers' seeds and core. Cut them into thin strips about ¼ in thick.

6- Drain the can of tuna, olives, and anchovies, and set aside.

7- Peel and slice the English cucumber into chunks or ½ inch-slices.

8- Place uncut lettuce leaves on a large shallow serving dish. Then place all ingredients attractively on top of the lettuce.

9-At the time of serving, drizzle with vinaigrette. Toss at the table in front of the guests.

Soufflé au Fromage

(Cheese Soufflé)

... Lola jerked up like a jack-in-the-box. "I can't make this. We're out of Parmesan."

"Substitute," Annie said.

"Substitute with what?"

"You could try cement. If the soufflé rises, it will make a very practical door stop." Suddenly the kitchen went silent. "What? What did I say?" She turned to see that Jared had entered the kitchen...

The Bois de Boulogne lake

Soufflé au Fromage -- Cheese Soufflé

There are many variables in soufflés that will be particular to your kitchen, elevation, your oven's personality, your mood... If you're preparing a soufflé for the first time I would recommend making it for your own ungrateful family first and only dare serve it to fancy company you're trying to impress when you've mastered it. Few dishes spell pathetic like a soufflé that won't rise.

The rule is: a soufflé doesn't wait for the guests, the guests wait for the soufflé.

Soufflé au Fromage -- Cheese Soufflé

Ingredients for four individual soufflés or one large one.

3 eggs at room temperature

1 cup (or 75 gr.) grated Gruyère cheese

2 tbsp unsalted butter

1tbsp flour

1 cup whole milk

Salt, pepper, and a pinch of nutmeg if desired

Directions

1-In a medium sauce pan, heat the butter on low heat until melted, then add the flour and stir briskly until slightly foamy but not brown. Remove from the heat and add all the milk.

Stir and place back on the stove. Add a very light touch of salt (you will soon be adding cheese) and pepper, and even a dash of nutmeg and stir gently until the mix is thick enough to coat a spoon.

Congratulations! You have just made béchamel sauce, the base for so many so-called 'cream sauces' in French cooking. Notice: no cream. Béchamel is in fact pretty lean. Although once you add the cheese and eggs further down this recipe...

2-Heat oven to 350°F. This recipe is for one regular soufflé mold (1 quart) or an oven-proof dish that is deep and circular (since there is apparently a law that states that square soufflés are in bad taste and violate laws of physics.) or 4 (round!) ramekins.

3-Separate the eggs whites from their yolks. Make sure no yolk gets into the whites or the soufflé might not rise. Using an electric mixer, or a hand-held electric blender (or by hand using a whisk, but only if you're a tennis player) beat the whites. Add a pinch of salt. Continue beating until the egg whites are firm enough that a spoon would stand straight when placed in the center.

4-The béchamel should still be warm enough that the cheese melts when you incorporate it. If not place it on the stove at very low heat for a minute, stirring. Away from the stove add the 3 egg yolks (which you didn't throw away because you are smart!)

5-With a wooden spoon, (not a whip or a fork), fold in the egg whites using a gentle, scooping, circular motion that will keep the mix foamy and not deflate the precious bubbles.

6-Pour the mix into the well-buttered soufflé mold (s). Place in the center of the oven and bake for 20 to 30 minutes or until the soufflé rises well past the top of the dish and is golden on top. Don't be too quick to remove it from the oven. Better to overcook than undercook so that the soufflé will not fall right away. It will fall eventually once you serve it, hopefully at the very moment your guests pierce it with their forks.

7-Serve with a green salad and homemade vinaigrette. No, you do not need to serve anything else with this dish, are you kidding? Have you counted the calories in this baby? Don't let the light as air appearance trick you into thinking it will also be light on the thighs.

Tartelettes aux Fruits

(Fruit Tartlets)

... Annie and the children walked back home and she listened to their day and let them talk her into a stop at the pâtisserie. *The strawberry* tartelettes *were ridiculously expensive with strawberries being so entirely out of season, but she said yes.*

"You said it was too expensive yesterday," Maxence pointed out.

"It's cheaper today."

"It's the same price. Look: 2.5 Euros each."

Annie sighed. "I'll have one too after all," she told the boulangère.

A painted ceiling at the Louvre.

Tartelettes aux Fruits -- Fruit Tartlets

The crispness of the brittle crust, the decadence of the cream, and the acidity of the fruit combine in irresistible ways in this traditional recipe. It's not hard to make but takes some time because of the separate steps and the need for the crust and crème filling to cool before assembly. The result will taste exactly like the tartelettes you can find in every boulangerie and patisserie in Paris.

Tartelettes aux Fruits -- Fruit Tartlets

Ingredients for one large tart or six small ones

Tart pans needed with removable bottoms! Non-stick is best -- if not remember to grease them.

Fruit

Fresh berries (strawberries, raspberries, blackberries) or drained canned fruit such as peaches, pears, apricots etc., or a combination.

Crust: Pâte à tarte

1 cup flour

1 egg yolk

4 tbsp unsalted butter, softened

1/3 cup granulated sugar

¼ tbsp salt

Cream filling: Crème pâtissière

1.5 cups milk

1/3 cup + 1 tbsp granulated sugar

1/3 cup white flour

2 egg yolks

1 tsp vanilla extract

A pinch of salt

Directions

Pâte à tarte: (crust)

1-Beat together softened (not melted) butter and sugar until creamy. Add the egg until completely incorporated. Add all flour and mix with your hands, rubbing the mix together rapidly. Do not work on this dough too long, only until everything is mixed. Roll the dough into a ball and place in the refrigerator for 30 minutes. This will harden the dough and make it 'spreadable'.

2- Preheat oven to 350° F.

3- Place the dough on a lightly floured surface. Using a rolling pin or your hands, flatten the dough to about ¼ in. thick. I'm no crust goddess, so I roll all my dough between two sheets of parchment paper, which makes everything a breeze; particularly the transfer of the dough to the pie mold. And remember: when it sticks, dust with flour.

4-Transfer the dough to the tart pan (s) (I keep my dough on the parchment paper and plop it in the pan.) Prick the dough with a fork so that it will cook evenly and won't bubble up.

5- Bake the pie crust for 10 to 15 minutes until slightly golden. Keep your eyes on it toward the end as it can go from golden to burned in an instant. Remove from the oven and let cool in dish.

Cream filling: Crème pâtissière

1-In a saucepan, bring the milk to a boil with the pinch of salt and the vanilla.

2- Meanwhile, in a medium bowl, whip the sugar and eggs together until smooth and lighter in color. Add flour slowly (I like to sift it through a fine mesh colander to avoid lumps, and it's so pretty!)

3- When the milk boils, pour it slowly into the bowl containing the sugar and flour mix. Adding too fast will result in the eggs cooking; you don't want that.

4- Pour the entire mixture back into the pan. Turn on the heat to medium low and cook as you whip the entire time. The mix will begin to thicken. Continue to cook for a minute after the first thickening. Do not let it stick to the saucepan.

5- Cover your crème pâtissière. Place it in the refrigerator until cooled off completely.

6- Assembly time! You've got your pie crusts (still in the pan), your crème pâtissière, and your fruit. Layer the cream at the bottom of the crust. Arrange the fruit prettily, remove from tart pan, and serve!

Another option is to heat up a tablespoon of berry jam in the microwave and brush over the fruit for that magical glow.

About the author

Corine Gantz was born in France, where she spent the first twenty years of her life. She studied Contemporary Arts at the Sorbonne, and has worked in advertising and marketing in Paris, San Francisco, and Los Angeles.

She self-published her first novel, Hidden in Paris, a story of friendship, love, food and dysfunction set in the City of Light in March 2011, and is currently working on a new novel also set in Paris.

She is the author of the popular blog Hidden in France where she uses her particular brand of humor to meditate on relationships, food, décor and all things French.

She lives near Los Angeles with her husband and their two sons.

Email her:

corinegantz@live.com

Visit her website:

www.corinegantz.com

Visit her blog:

www.hiddeninfrance.typepad.com

This is a work of fiction. Any resemblance of characters to actual persons (or vegetable, fruit, mammals and amphibians), living or dead, is purely coincidental.

For information, email:

corinegantz@live.com

Hidden in Paris—The Cookbook

Carpenter Hill Publishing

ISBN-10: 0983436622

ISBN-13: 978-0-9834366-2-1

A note by the author

Many of you have chosen this cookbook because you read Hidden in Paris, liked it and wanted more. Thank you for sharing the fun with me. I'm thrilled you are here!

Writing in my little room (and by little I mean precisely 8 x 8 feet), alone and without the support and connection of other writers, I struggled for years with nagging thoughts such as "do I have the right to call myself a writer?", "is this English of Franglish I'm writing in?" and "do NOT think of the package of Milano cookies you hid way in the back of the cupboard." But above all I struggled with fear. Fear that Hidden in Paris would be a flop and that it would turn me off to writing. Fear that I would not be able to give readers the kind of pleasure I experience when a novel manages to transport me entirely to another place. Fear that bad reviews would drill holes through my insecure heart. At the time I had no readership to speak of, aside from loyal blogging friends who wanted to spread the word and did so enthusiastically as soon as the novel was out.

Amazingly, shame and failure did not happen. Better yet: readers who loved the book wrote fantastic reviews that made me cry (all right... I cried over the negative reviews too, but surprisingly they did not kill me), Bloggers worked their magic... and Amazon, Barnes and Nobles, iTunes and many awesome independent book stores did the rest. The novel gained momentum and now sells in a way that makes me smile every day. Hidden in Paris is not a best seller, it is not advertised in the New York Times and Oprah will never review it, but I now get to be a full time, self-employed writer. Sure the boss is a slave driver but I can't think of a greater job. Freedom, my friends, is sweet. And for this amazing break in my life, I have all of you, my readers, to thank.

If you find typos and errors in this cookbook please send an email to yell at me at corinegantz@live.com. I'll correct them right away and will credit you on my website if you'll allow me. And if you want to write a nice review on Amazon or elsewhere you will have my undying gratitude.

Thank you so very much beloved readers, from the bottom of my heart.

Acknowledgements

Many thanks to Jennifer Herron, a perfect stranger at the time, who found over thirty typos in Hidden in Paris long after it was printed and everyone else had given up on the task. I was so impressed by her kindness and talent that I begged her to help me proofread this cookbook. She was lovely enough to say yes (it helps that she's a foodie).You rock Jennifer!

If you want to get in contact with her for any proofreading and editing, please send an email to jenthr@eartlink.net.

Thank you to my husband Joe for being wildly enthusiastic about everything I cook, even when it's really bad. Thank you to David for missing your *maman's* cooking while in college, and thank you Nathan, the skeptical eater in our family for trying a minuscule bit of that 'weird chicken' I made the other day. By the way, honey: it was fish!

"In a tale of friendship, self-discovery and love, three women running away from their lives become unlikely friends in a beautiful house in the heart of Paris."

Hidden in Paris, synopsis

Lost in France, a country she mistrusts, among French people she hardly understands, Annie has trouble venturing away from home since the death of her husband. And since home happens to be a small jewel of a house nestled in the heart of Paris, why would she ever want to? But when bankruptcy threatens her beloved house, her one anchor in life, Annie has no choice but to find renters, and quick.

Leave it to someone socially phobic to phrase a want ad in all the wrong ways. With shimmering promises of 'Starting over in Paris' — a concept she has no intention of applying to her own life—Annie attracts tenants with the kind of baggage that doesn't fit in suitcases. A long-legged, coolheaded ex model (everything Annie is definitely not) on the run from her abusive husband, a frail young woman harboring a possible death wish, a mysterious French artist, and an infuriating blue-blooded French man soon threaten Annie's way of life in ways she never anticipated.

But when Annie finds herself reluctantly yet actively engaged in the rescue of her tenants, she discovers that she might just save herself in the process.

What readers are saying about Hidden in Paris

" I was sick this cold, snowy weekend so I decided to load something to my iPad from Amazon searching under the heading "France" and stumbled across this gem, Hidden in Paris. What a treat! As a teen, I spent many summers in Paris and have continued my love affair with the city over twenty years later. I read all day AND night and finished the book this morning. While i really enjoyed the story of how the women's lives changed, the author had me the minute she described the location. How I wish I could live in such an amazing house, on that street deep in the heart of Paris. This book makes me long to go back in time for next year's Fete de la Musique.

Beatrice, Amazon review

"I loved how the author allowed me to feel and be part of the chaos. I loved how with each page, I was able to see clearer into the story told. It was simple, whimsical, and naked in the way raw emotion sometimes is. I "felt" a lot reading this book. This book said to me that all hell breaks loose for a reason and when that reason is unveiled, it's worth the trouble."

LivFst, Amazon review

"This is one of the best books I've read in quite awhile! The location is so authentic and if you close your eyes you really feel like you are on the streets of Paris! The author's characters are so realistic that I actually felt like I knew these people. Obviously the author's knowledge of Paris comes from personal experience not just research. This is definitely a "feel good" story! I eagerly await another novel from this author."

book crazy, Amazon review

"I finished this book last night and found it really a great read. Was transported back to Paris and the characters in the book were so enjoyable. When I finished I wanted to read more about everyone - could have just kept going.

A really great first novel."

Jayell, Amazon review

"...I made a prediction that I wasn't going to like it. What a stupid thing to do. It took me awhile to read the first 30 pages or so and then I was hooked. I couldn't put it down, I took it everywhere with me, much to my children's dismay.

The characters were delightful, bad, good and in-between. I wanted to hate Mark, but the way he was portrayed I just knew he wasn't all bad and there was hope for him yet. I also wanted to label Lucas as a womanizing French snob but again, the way Ms. Gantz described him, I knew there was more to him than met the eye. Jared was a mystery and a surprise altogether. Althea's situation was heartbreaking, I wanted find her mother and punch her in the nose. Lola and Annie were fun and reminded me of some of my friends from my single days. When you have a talented writer like Ms. Gantz to develop and put all these characters together with such a clever storyline you have one hell of a novel.

The storyline kept me interested, it was not at all predictable and as I said before I couldn't put it down once I got started. Ms. Gantz has the ability to make you fall in love with a location and its inhabitants to the point that you wish they were real so you could make a visit!"

Tracie, goodreads review

I have fallen in love with a house, three women, two men and five children. I have fallen in love with this book. The author brings her characters to life and you find yourself not only liking them but rooting for them. You want the happy ending. You meet Annie, the mother of three young boys, whose husband died three years ago. She uses her home and food as permanent occupations for the time her sons are in school. She renovates the house and cooks wonderful meals to fill her days but now money is running out and she needs to think what to do. Filled with her own insecurities, she now fills her home with roomers with insecurities. Lola, the former model turned mother of two, escapes from her husband and perfect California life. She arrives in Paris with her children and finds a hiding place in Annie's home. Althea flees a loneliness that has trapped her and taken hold of her life. Jared has his own demons to escape. Then there is Lucas, Jared's godfather and

Annie's best friend. You will come to know these people and will at times like and dislike them and the decisions they make but they will keep you interested.

I laughed out loud and even shed a tear. There is no perfect happy ever after in life but this book leaves you hoping there could be.

Karen M. Amazon review

"...I loved this book! I know you're not supposed to judge a book by its cover, but with this one, you should do just that! The beautiful picture on the front opens up to a wonderfully rich, beautiful and inspiring slice of life, set in Paris, which makes it even better! You'll fall in love with each of the characters in this book, they are all very human, with problems we can all relate to in some way. This is a story of old hurts, new beginnings, friendships and love, and fresh hope for the future. I recommend this book very highly!"

Cathy, goodreads review

"I loved Hidden in Paris! Ms. Gantz has created a story that should be read and savored - much like the Parisian lifestyle she depicts. The characters were deep and immensely likable and the plot line was smooth and delicious. They say every writer has one great novel inside them somewhere. Well, I dearly hope Ms. Gantz has another one to follow up this masterpiece! The undertones of love and motherhood, self-loathing and hidden anger are so palpable that it's bound to keep readers up way past their bedtimes. Truly, truly, truly an excellent novel that leaves its reader pondering the characters' lives and choices long after the last page. I'd recommend this book to anyone and everyone!"

Megan, Amazon review

"This book makes me want to go back to France! The food! The unique people! I love the characters in Corine Gantz's book, they aren't perfect or one dimensional. Each one has their struggles but they come out on top. I love the romance between Annie and Lucas. Beautiful book cover!"

Susan, goodreads review

"...Everything I have been missing about Paris is in it (the good things about the French as well as the annoying ones!). I got attached to the characters right away, I like that they were multi dimensional (how boring when everyone is either wonderful or evil with no in between). It made me want to move into that beautiful house and be nurtured by Annie and fed her amazing cooking. This book makes you travel to France without having to buy a plane ticket."

Isabelle, goodreads review

"...What's more precious than several hours of private reading pleasure? Especially if you're lucky enough to have a book that draws you into the characters the way "Hidden in Paris" does. Reading the book I saw a little piece of myself in every female character and they reminded me of my own circle of wildly disparate friends, too. These characters come off as real people with real problems but they all have a great deal of heart.."

Fengshui by Fishgirl, goodreads review

"I was attracted to this author's blog by looking at interior design/style websites. I visit frequently and was thrilled that her book was complete and downloaded the Kindle version instantly. True to form, the yarn is spun smoothly and stylishly, with humor. While getting to know the characters, you get to visit France and taste the food! ~Each event, conflict and individual that enters and leaves in a life, are significant pieces of a unique mosaic. This was beautifully demonstrated in this lovely story."

Julie, Amazon review

Reading some of the reviews, I was mystified. Researching the critics, I found all but one liked very little they had purchased. Sounds more like home buyer's remorse addiction than an honest critique of "Hidden in Paris" (or anything else they purchased). The other is a young, self-proclaimed critic with a web site. No criticism on my part as everyone needs a niche. I just like to see who is critiquing. Myself, I have no credentials, but loved the book. I bought it on my Kindle ... by accident, hitting the wrong title. I wish all my mistakes turned out this well. The creativity, fluidity, humor and unique writing style make this a first-rate read. The characters are live and real, pulling few punches. You may not like this if you are dealing with some of the real character issues or have a history you are trying to forget. For myself, I found the "realness" of characters added a welcome balance to many other books I have read where the characters' problems lag with superficiality. This being said, I found most of the characters fun and intriguing. This leaves me with a question: When is Corine Gantz publishing her next? "Hidden in Paris" is a very good first novel.

Oubliable "Tim," Amazon review

I truly enjoyed this book and all it's quirky characters. Yes, things turn out the way you want them to and expect them to, but is that such a bad deal? I didn't realize it was self-published until the very end which makes me like it even more and gain much respect for the author for following her own dream. It would make a wonderful movie.

Betsy, Amazon review

I really enjoyed this book. I have never been to Paris and now I feel like I have. Before purchasing this book, I read all the reviews and even though a couple people didn't enjoy it, I figured it must not be there type of genre. The fact that the characters have personal issues they are dealing with makes the story even more intriguing. I cannot wait until Mrs. Gantz writes another book.

Serenity17, Amazon review

I purchased this book on a whim because my husband and I were going to Paris in August, and I am really glad I did. I loved the characters, I loved the insight into the personalities of Parisians, and I really loved the descriptions of Annie's food! I think there should be a follow-up cookbook...

M. Napoli, Amazon review

ISBN: **0983436622**

ISBN-13: **978-0983436621**

Printed in Great Britain
by Amazon

70573737R00054